Overflowing

with

Gratitude

Expanded Version

Leaning In
to your

Lifestyle of
Gratitude

Overflowing with Gratitude

Copyright © 2019 Gina Low

Gratitude, Self-Awareness, Self-Development, Personal Growth, Happiness

Cover and interior design by Gina Low

ISBN: 9781699901267

Printed in the United States of America

Disclaimer: This publication is sold with the understanding that the author is not engaged in rendering professional psychological services. If expert assistance or counseling is needed, the services of a competent professional should be sought.

We are what we repeatedly do.
Excellence, then, is not an act, but a
habit.

Aristotle

Version 2 of the **Overflowing with Gratitude** journal was specifically created with the seasoned journaler in mind – someone looking to get a little more detailed in thoughts and a little more intentional in daily practices. DON'T WORRY, though, if you're new! The levels of self-analysis required are incremental by design; as long as you're committed, the process will work for you!

> "It is said that 21 days of consistent behavior will make or break a habit, but social science is proving that this common theory is far too simplistic. It really is what you do every day after that creates a desired lifestyle. Research now shows that an average of 60+ days of repetition is required for something to become habitual, and at least 90 days for auto-pilot to take over. Ninety days to create a lifestyle. Three months. One quarter of one year to create a drastically different lifestyle for yourself."
> *(from original version)*

The main principal behind using gratitude to change your life is to just BE Grateful. There is no better catalyst for an attitude of gratitude than documenting the things/people/moments for which you're thankful. Building a habit of documenting three specific things daily works in several ways, but most importantly to turn your full attention to each item. When you're focused on the mental imagery presented by each, your brain returns those feelings as if you were reliving that moment.

This expanded version includes the basics of documentation, but also launches further into activities and processes that aid in BEing Grateful. To BE is a verb meaning "to equal". In order to *equal* Gratitude, those thankful feelings must be expressed and lived.

Because *awareness* is the first and possibly most important step to creating the life you desire, this journal includes built-in benchmarks to note both physical and emotional attributes of each day. Conscious recognition and acceptance of your current state of being creates the opportunity to make changes in behavior and beliefs.

Where your Attention Goes, your Energy Flows

You may note a less than positive mood, but there's no writing space provided to note the details. Changing your mindset around a particular mood or feeling is much easier to do BEFORE the momentum of emotion has taken control. Note the undesired feeling, then quickly move your focus toward the positive. If necessary, use Gabrielle Bernstein's *"Choose Again"* method. Turn your focus unto *anything* that brings you joy, feel that feeling, and let your perception instantly shift.

YOU Decide

Set your intention daily. How will you honor yourself? With what feeling will you CHOOSE to label your day? What will you decide to accomplish? Things as little as drinking enough water, and as big as conquering the mountain of laundry - there is nothing un-important about what you choose to accomplish. Intentional prioritization helps build awareness about how the choices you make affect the bigger picture.

Your thoughts will determine the outcomes in your life. I invite you to Lean In to this adventure, exploring and adjusting your thoughts - begin to notice the little things that make you smile each day.

Be Grateful; Be Love.

Be grateful
for your life,
every detail of it,
and your face
will come to
shine like the sun,
and everyone
who sees it
will be made
glad and peaceful.

Persist in gratitude,
and you will slowly
become one
with the
Sun of Love,
and Love will shine
through you
it's all-healing joy.

-Rumi

TRADE YOUR EXPECTATIONS FOR APPRECIATION,
AND YOUR WHOLE WORLD CHANGES IN AN INSTANT.

-TONY ROBBINS

Week

1

_____ to _____

This week I am most excited about:

_____

_____

_____

_____

This week I plan to Thank Myself by:

_____

_____

_____

_____

Week1 | Day1 _____, 20_____

My mood this morning is: _____.

I slept: □ well   □ not well
             □ long enough   □ not long enough

My day is going to be: _____!

Evening Attitude Check: ___ *positive* ___*negative*

Today, I honored my physical being by:

_____

_____

Today, I accomplished:

_____

_____

My choice to accomplish _____
supports the life I am trying to create by:

_____

_____

Today, I was most thankful for:

_____

_____

_____

_____

_____

_____

_____

_____

_____

_____

_____

_____

_____

_____

_____

Tomorrow, I intend to have a _____ *day, full*
of _____ *!*

Week1 | Day2   _____, 20_____

My mood this morning is: _____.

I slept: □ well   □ not well

                  □ long enough   □ not long enough

My day is going to be: _____!

Evening Attitude Check: ___ positive   ___negative

Today, I honored my physical being by:

_____

_____

Today, I accomplished:

_____

_____

My choice to accomplish _____

supports the life I am trying to create by:

_____

_____

Today, I was most thankful for:

_____

_____

_____

_____

_____

_____

_____

_____

_____

_____

_____

_____

_____

_____

_____

Tomorrow, I intend to have a _____ **day, full of** _____ **!**

Week1 | Day3 _____, 20_____

My mood this morning is: _____.

I slept: □ well □ not well
□ long enough □ not long enough

My day is going to be: _____!

Evening Attitude Check: ___ *positive* ___*negative*

Today, I honored my physical being by:

_____

_____

Today, I accomplished:

_____

_____

My choice to accomplish _____

supports the life I am trying to create by:

_____

_____

Today, I was most thankful for:

_____

_____

_____

_____

_____

_____

_____

_____

_____

_____

_____

_____

_____

_____

Tomorrow, I intend to have a _____ *day, full of* _____ *!*

Week1 | Day4 _____, 20_____

My mood this morning is: _____.

I slept: □ well   □ not well
          □ long enough □ not long enough

My day is going to be: _____!

Evening Attitude Check: ___ *positive*   ___*negative*

Today, I honored my physical being by:

_____

_____

Today, I accomplished:

_____

_____

My choice to accomplish _____

supports the life I am trying to create by:

_____

_____

Today, I was most thankful for:

_____

_____

_____

_____

_____

_____

_____

_____

_____

_____

_____

_____

_____

_____

Tomorrow, I intend to have a _____ *day, full*

of _____ *!*

Week1 | Day5   _____, 20_____

My mood this morning is: _____.

I slept: □ well   □ not well
                 □ long enough   □ not long enough

My day is going to be: _____!

Evening Attitude Check: ___ *positive*   ___*negative*

Today, I honored my physical being by:

_____

_____

Today, I accomplished:

_____

_____

My choice to accomplish _____

supports the life I am trying to create by:

_____

_____

Today, I was most thankful for:

_____

_____

_____

_____

_____

_____

_____

_____

_____

_____

_____

_____

_____

_____

_____

Tomorrow, I intend to have a _____**day, full of** _____**!**

Week1 | Day6 _____, 20_____

My mood this morning is: _____.

I slept: □ well   □ not well
             □ long enough   □ not long enough

My day is going to be: _____!

Evening Attitude Check: ___ *positive*   ___*negative*

Today, I honored my physical being by:

_____

_____

Today, I accomplished:

_____

_____

My choice to accomplish _____

supports the life I am trying to create by:

_____

_____

Today, I was most thankful for:

_____

_____

_____

_____

_____

_____

_____

_____

_____

_____

_____

_____

_____

_____

_____

Tomorrow, I intend to have a _____ **day, full**

of _____ **!**

Week1 | Day7   _____, 20_____

My mood this morning is: _____.

I slept: □ well   □ not well
               □ long enough   □ not long enough

My day is going to be: _____!

Evening Attitude Check: ___ *positive*   ___*negative*

Today, I honored my physical being by:

_____

_____

Today, I accomplished:

_____

_____

My choice to accomplish _____

supports the life I am trying to create by:

_____

_____

Today, I was most thankful for:

_____

_____

_____

_____

_____

_____

_____

_____

_____

_____

_____

_____

_____

_____

Tomorrow, I intend to have a _____day, full

of _____!

Weekly Reflection #1

If you're new to this, it can sometimes be challenging to think of or recall three - even more difficult to write about DIFFERENT things every day, and as you proceed, even more difficult to get specific and detailed. How difficult has it been to write about three things every day? Do you notice things you love about your environment? Are you staying present in the moments?

_____

_____

_____

_____

_____

_____

_____

_____

_____

_____

_____

_____

_____

_____

_____

_____

_____

_____

_____

_____

_____

_____

_____

_____

_____

_____

_____

_____

Pro Tips:

1. Set alarms for am & pm journaling.
2. If you have more than 3, use the NOTES section in the back to build a reserve of "extras" you can use the next day.
3. Don't let this get overwhelming; the main purpose is building a habit. The benefits of practice will continue to multiply.

GRATITUDE OPENS THE DOOR TO THE POWER, THE WISDOM,
THE CREATIVITY OF THE UNIVERSE.

-DEEPAK CHOPRA

Week

2

_____ to _____

This week I am most excited about:

_____

_____

_____

_____

This week I plan to Thank Myself by:

_____

_____

_____

_____

Week2 | Day1   _____, 20_____

My mood this morning is: _____.

I slept: □ well   □ not well
             □ long enough   □ not long enough

My day is going to be: _____!

Evening Attitude Check: ___ *positive*   ___*negative*

Today, I honored my physical being by:

_____

_____

Today, I accomplished:

_____

_____

My choice to accomplish _____

supports the life I am trying to create by:

_____

_____

Today, I was most thankful for:

_____

_____

_____

_____

_____

_____

_____

_____

_____

_____

_____

_____

_____

_____

_____

Tomorrow, I intend to have a _____ *day, full*

of _____ *!*

Week2 | Day2   _____, 20_____

My mood this morning is: _____.

I slept: □ well   □ not well
                 □ long enough   □ not long enough

My day is going to be: _____!

Evening Attitude Check: ___ *positive*   ___*negative*

Today, I honored my physical being by:

_____

_____

Today, I accomplished:

_____

_____

My choice to accomplish _____

supports the life I am trying to create by:

_____

_____

Today, I was most thankful for:

_____

_____

_____

_____

_____

_____

_____

_____

_____

_____

_____

_____

_____

_____

_____

Tomorrow, I intend to have a _____ *day, full*

of _____*!*

Week2 | Day3 _____, 20_____

My mood this morning is: _____.

I slept: □ well   □ not well
                 □ long enough   □ not long enough

My day is going to be: _____!

Evening Attitude Check: ___ *positive* ___*negative*

Today, I honored my physical being by:

_____

_____

Today, I accomplished:

_____

_____

My choice to accomplish _____

supports the life I am trying to create by:

_____

_____

Today, I was most thankful for:

_____

_____

_____

_____

_____

_____

_____

_____

_____

_____

_____

_____

_____

_____

Tomorrow, I intend to have a _____ **day, full**
of _____ **!**

Week2 | Day4 _____ , 20_____

My mood this morning is: _____.

I slept: □ well □ not well
          □ long enough □ not long enough

My day is going to be: _____!

Evening Attitude Check: ___ *positive* ___*negative*

Today, I honored my physical being by:

_____

_____

Today, I accomplished:

_____

_____

My choice to accomplish _____
supports the life I am trying to create by:

_____

_____

Today, I was most thankful for:

_____

_____

_____

_____

_____

_____

_____

_____

_____

_____

_____

_____

_____

_____

Tomorrow, I intend to have a _____ **day, full**

of _____ **!**

Week2 | Day5 _____, 20_____

My mood this morning is: _____.

I slept: □ well   □ not well
          □ long enough   □ not long enough

My day is going to be: _____!

Evening Attitude Check: ___ *positive*   ___*negative*

Today, I honored my physical being by:

_____

_____

Today, I accomplished:

_____

_____

My choice to accomplish _____

supports the life I am trying to create by:

_____

_____

Today, I was most thankful for:

_____

_____

_____

_____

_____

_____

_____

_____

_____

_____

_____

_____

_____

_____

_____

Tomorrow, I intend to have a _____ **day, full**

of _____**!**

Week2 | Day6 _____, 20_____

My mood this morning is: _____.

I slept: □ well   □ not well
             □ long enough   □ not long enough

My day is going to be: _____!

Evening Attitude Check: ___ *positive*   ___*negative*

Today, I honored my physical being by:

_____

_____

Today, I accomplished:

_____

_____

My choice to accomplish _____

supports the life I am trying to create by:

_____

_____

Today, I was most thankful for:

_____

_____

_____

_____

_____

_____

_____

_____

_____

_____

_____

_____

_____

_____

_____

Tomorrow, I intend to have a _____ **day, full of** _____ **!**

Week2 | Day7 _____, 20_____

My mood this morning is: _____.

I slept: □ well   □ not well
             □ long enough   □ not long enough

My day is going to be: _____!

Evening Attitude Check: ___ *positive*   ___*negative*

Today, I honored my physical being by:

_____

_____

Today, I accomplished:

_____

_____

My choice to accomplish _____

supports the life I am trying to create by:

_____

_____

Today, I was most thankful for:

_____

_____

_____

_____

_____

_____

_____

_____

_____

_____

_____

_____

_____

_____

Tomorrow, I intend to have a _____*day, full*

of _____*!*

Weekly Reflection #2

Hopefully you've noticed the heavy use of self-determination throughout this journal. Every morning, after noting a "current" mood, you are asked to make a decision about the feeling you'd like to have throughout your day. Every evening, you have a quick attitude check, and make another decision about the outlook you have on the following day. Have you noticed if/how this process has affected your actual mood? Are your "current status" check-ins aligning with your declarations? When someone asks how you're doing, do you respond accordingly?

_____

_____

_____

_____

_____

_____

_____

_____

_____

_____

GRATITUDE IS AN ESSENTIAL PART OF BEING PRESENT. WHEN YOU GO DEEPLY INTO THE PRESENT, GRATITUDE ARISES SPONTANEOUSLY.

-EKHART TOLLE

Week

3

_____ to _____

This week I am most excited about:

_____

_____

_____

_____

This week I plan to Thank Myself by:

_____

_____

_____

_____

Week3 | Day1   _____, 20_____

My mood this morning is: _____.

I slept: □ well   □ not well
              □ long enough   □ not long enough

My day is going to be: _____!

Evening Attitude Check: ___ *positive*   ___*negative*

Today, I honored my physical being by:

_____

_____

Today, I accomplished:

_____

_____

My choice to accomplish _____

supports the life I am trying to create by:

_____

_____

Today, I was most thankful for:

_____

_____

_____

_____

_____

_____

_____

_____

_____

_____

_____

_____

_____

_____

_____

Tomorrow, I intend to have a _____ **day, full**

of _____ **!**

Week3 | Day2 _____, 20_____

My mood this morning is: _____.

I slept: □ well   □ not well
          □ long enough   □ not long enough

My day is going to be: _____!

Evening Attitude Check: ___ *positive*   ___*negative*

Today, I honored my physical being by:

_____

_____

Today, I accomplished:

_____

_____

My choice to accomplish _____

supports the life I am trying to create by:

_____

_____

Today, I was most thankful for:

_____

_____

_____

_____

_____

_____

_____

_____

_____

_____

_____

_____

_____

_____

Tomorrow, I intend to have a _____**day, full**

of _____**!**

Week3 | Day3 _____, 20_____

My mood this morning is: _____.

I slept: □ well   □ not well
                □ long enough   □ not long enough

My day is going to be: _____!

Evening Attitude Check: ___ *positive*   ___*negative*

Today, I honored my physical being by:

_____

_____

Today, I accomplished:

_____

_____

My choice to accomplish _____

supports the life I am trying to create by:

_____

_____

Today, I was most thankful for:

_____

_____

_____

_____

_____

_____

_____

_____

_____

_____

_____

_____

_____

_____

Tomorrow, I intend to have a _____ **day, full of** _____ **!**

Week3 | Day4 _____, 20_____

My mood this morning is: _____.

I slept: ☐ well ☐ not well
☐ long enough ☐ not long enough

My day is going to be: _____!

Evening Attitude Check: ___ *positive* ___*negative*

Today, I honored my physical being by:

_____

_____

Today, I accomplished:

_____

_____

My choice to accomplish _____

supports the life I am trying to create by:

_____

_____

Today, I was most thankful for:

_____

_____

_____

_____

_____

_____

_____

_____

_____

_____

_____

_____

_____

_____

Tomorrow, I intend to have a _____ *day, full*

of _____ *!*

Week3 | Day5 _____, 20_____

My mood this morning is: _____.

I slept: □ well   □ not well
          □ long enough   □ not long enough

My day is going to be: _____!

Evening Attitude Check: ___ *positive*   ___*negative*

Today, I honored my physical being by:

_____

_____

Today, I accomplished:

_____

_____

My choice to accomplish _____

supports the life I am trying to create by:

_____

_____

Today, I was most thankful for:

_____

_____

_____

_____

_____

_____

_____

_____

_____

_____

_____

_____

_____

_____

_____

Tomorrow, I intend to have a _____*day, full*
of _____*!*

Week3 | Day6   _____, 20_____

My mood this morning is: _____.

I slept: □ well   □ not well
                   □ long enough   □ not long enough

My day is going to be: _____!

Evening Attitude Check: ___ *positive*   ___*negative*

Today, I honored my physical being by:

_____

_____

Today, I accomplished:

_____

_____

My choice to accomplish _____

supports the life I am trying to create by:

_____

_____

Today, I was most thankful for:

_____

_____

_____

_____

_____

_____

_____

_____

_____

_____

_____

_____

_____

_____

Tomorrow, I intend to have a _____**day, full**
of _____**!**

Week3 | Day7   _____, 20_____

My mood this morning is: _____.

I slept: □ well   □ not well
              □ long enough   □ not long enough

My day is going to be: _____!

Evening Attitude Check: ___ *positive*   ___*negative*

Today, I honored my physical being by:

_____

_____

Today, I accomplished:

_____

_____

My choice to accomplish _____

supports the life I am trying to create by:

_____

_____

Today, I was most thankful for:

_____

_____

_____

_____

_____

_____

_____

_____

_____

_____

_____

_____

_____

_____

Tomorrow, I intend to have a _____ *day, full*
of _____ *!*

Weekly Reflection #3

Learning to make gratitude a lifestyle is a process. Our programming is to thank external sources, and that really is important. What is also important is learning to THANK OURSELVES. Your body, your mind, your heart – they all provide high-quality functions every single day. How has being intentional about thanking yourself affected your well-being? Do you notice this affecting your self-worth? Has it had any effect on how you show up in the world?

THE STRUGGLE ENDS WHERE GRATITUDE BEGINS.

-NEALE DONALD WALSCH

Week

4

_____ to _____

This week I am most excited about:

_____

_____

_____

_____

This week I plan to Thank Myself by:

_____

_____

_____

_____

Week4 | Day1   _____, 20_____

My mood this morning is: _____.

I slept: □ well   □ not well
                  □ long enough   □ not long enough

My day is going to be: _____!

Evening Attitude Check: ___ *positive*   ___*negative*

Today, I honored my physical being by:

_____

_____

Today, I accomplished:

_____

_____

My choice to accomplish _____

supports the life I am trying to create by:

_____

_____

Today, I was most thankful for:

_____

_____

_____

_____

_____

_____

_____

_____

_____

_____

_____

_____

_____

Tomorrow, I intend to have a _____ **day, full**

of _____ **!**

Week4 | Day2 _____, 20_____

My mood this morning is: _____.

I slept: □ well   □ not well
             □ long enough   □ not long enough

My day is going to be: _____!

Evening Attitude Check: ___ *positive* ___*negative*

Today, I honored my physical being by:

_____

_____

Today, I accomplished:

_____

_____

My choice to accomplish _____

supports the life I am trying to create by:

_____

_____

Today, I was most thankful for:

_____

_____

_____

_____

_____

_____

_____

_____

_____

_____

_____

_____

_____

_____

Tomorrow, I intend to have a _____ *day, full*

of _____ *!*

Week4 | Day3 _____, 20_____

My mood this morning is: _____.

I slept: □ well   □ not well
          □ long enough   □ not long enough

My day is going to be: _____!

Evening Attitude Check: ___ *positive*   ___*negative*

Today, I honored my physical being by:

_____

_____

Today, I accomplished:

_____

_____

My choice to accomplish _____

supports the life I am trying to create by:

_____

_____

Today, I was most thankful for:

_____

_____

_____

_____

_____

_____

_____

_____

_____

_____

_____

_____

_____

_____

Tomorrow, I intend to have a _____ **day, full**
of _____ **!**

Week4 | Day4   _____, 20_____

My mood this morning is: _____.

I slept: □ well   □ not well
                □ long enough   □ not long enough

My day is going to be: _____!

Evening Attitude Check: ___ *positive*   ___*negative*

Today, I honored my physical being by:

_____

_____

Today, I accomplished:

_____

_____

My choice to accomplish _____

supports the life I am trying to create by:

_____

_____

Today, I was most thankful for:

_____

_____

_____

_____

_____

.

_____

_____

_____

_____

_____

_____

_____

_____

_____

_____

Tomorrow, I intend to have a _____**day, full**

of _____**!**

Week4 | Day5 _____, 20_____

My mood this morning is: _____.

I slept: □ well □ not well
          □ long enough □ not long enough

My day is going to be: _____!

Evening Attitude Check: ___ *positive* ___*negative*

Today, I honored my physical being by:

_____

_____

Today, I accomplished:

_____

_____

My choice to accomplish _____
supports the life I am trying to create by:

_____

_____

Today, I was most thankful for:

_____

_____

_____

_____

_____

_____

_____

_____

_____

_____

_____

_____

_____

_____

_____

Tomorrow, I intend to have a _____ **day, full
of** _____ **!**

Week4 | Day6 _____, 20_____

My mood this morning is: _____.

I slept: □ well   □ not well
          □ long enough   □ not long enough

My day is going to be: _____!

Evening Attitude Check: ___ *positive* ___*negative*

Today, I honored my physical being by:

_____

_____

Today, I accomplished:

_____

_____

My choice to accomplish _____

supports the life I am trying to create by:

_____

_____

Today, I was most thankful for:

_____

_____

_____

_____

_____

_____

_____

_____

_____

_____

_____

_____

_____

_____

_____

Tomorrow, I intend to have a _____ *day, full*
of _____ *!*

Week4 | Day7 _____, 20_____

My mood this morning is: _____.

I slept: □ well   □ not well
              □ long enough   □ not long enough

My day is going to be: _____!

Evening Attitude Check: ___ *positive* ___*negative*

Today, I honored my physical being by:

_____

_____

Today, I accomplished:

_____

_____

My choice to accomplish _____

supports the life I am trying to create by:

_____

_____

Today, I was most thankful for:

_____

_____

_____

_____

_____

_____

_____

_____

_____

_____

_____

_____

_____

_____

_____

Tomorrow, I intend to have a _____ day, full of _____ !

Weekly Reflection #4

Holistic wellness integrates the health of the mind, body, and soul. Just as physical exercise alone cannot create whole-health, it is important to honor your physical being as you focus on your spiritual wellness. What habits are you creating to honor yourself physically, and do you notice how this has affected your daily life? Do you have more clarity? Sleep better? Feel more energetic? Are you more conscientious about how you treat your body?

_____

_____

_____

_____

_____

_____

_____

_____

_____

_____

APPRECIATION IS A WONDERFUL THING.
IT MAKES WHAT IS EXCELLENT IN OTHERS BECOME OURS AS WELL.

-VOLTAIRE

Week

5

_____ to _____

This week I am most excited about:

_____

_____

_____

_____

This week I plan to Thank Myself by:

_____

_____

_____

_____

Week5 | Day1 _____, 20_____

My mood this morning is: _____.

I slept: □ well   □ not well
             □ long enough   □ not long enough

My day is going to be: _____!

Evening Attitude Check: ___ *positive* ___*negative*

Today, I honored my physical being by:

_____

_____

Today, I accomplished:

_____

_____

My choice to accomplish _____

supports the life I am trying to create by:

_____

_____

Today, I was most thankful for:

_____

_____

_____

_____

_____

_____

_____

_____

_____

_____

_____

_____

_____

_____

Tomorrow, I intend to have a _____ **day, full**
of _____ **!**

Week5 | Day2 _____, 20_____

My mood this morning is: _____.

I slept: □ well   □ not well
                □ long enough   □ not long enough

My day is going to be: _____!

Evening Attitude Check: ___ *positive*   ___*negative*

Today, I honored my physical being by:

_____

_____

Today, I accomplished:

_____

_____

My choice to accomplish _____

supports the life I am trying to create by:

_____

_____

Today, I was most thankful for:

_____

_____

_____

_____

_____

_____

_____

_____

_____

_____

_____

_____

_____

_____

_____

Tomorrow, I intend to have a _____ *day, full*

of _____ *!*

Week5 | Day3 _____, 20_____

My mood this morning is: _____.

I slept: □ well   □ not well
               □ long enough   □ not long enough

My day is going to be: _____!

Evening Attitude Check: ___ *positive*   ___*negative*

Today, I honored my physical being by:

_____

_____

Today, I accomplished:

_____

_____

My choice to accomplish _____

supports the life I am trying to create by:

_____

_____

Today, I was most thankful for:

_____

_____

_____

_____

_____

_____

_____

_____

_____

_____

_____

_____

_____

_____

Tomorrow, I intend to have a _____ **day, full of** _____ **!**

Week5 | Day4 _____, 20_____

My mood this morning is: _____.

I slept: □ well   □ not well
          □ long enough   □ not long enough

My day is going to be: _____!

Evening Attitude Check: ___ *positive*   ___*negative*

Today, I honored my physical being by:

_____

_____

Today, I accomplished:

_____

_____

My choice to accomplish _____

supports the life I am trying to create by:

_____

_____

Today, I was most thankful for:

_____

_____

_____

_____

_____

_____

_____

_____

_____

_____

_____

_____

_____

_____

Tomorrow, I intend to have a _____ **day, full**
of _____ **!**

Week5 | Day5 _____, 20_____

My mood this morning is: _____.

I slept: □ well   □ not well
          □ long enough   □ not long enough

My day is going to be: _____!

Evening Attitude Check: ___ *positive* ___*negative*

Today, I honored my physical being by:

_____

_____

Today, I accomplished:

_____

_____

My choice to accomplish _____

supports the life I am trying to create by:

_____

_____

Today, I was most thankful for:

_____

_____

_____

_____

_____

_____

_____

_____

_____

_____

_____

_____

_____

_____

Tomorrow, I intend to have a _____ *day, full*

of _____ *!*

Week5 | Day6 _____, 20_____

My mood this morning is: _____.

I slept: □ well   □ not well
          □ long enough   □ not long enough

My day is going to be: _____!

Evening Attitude Check: ___ *positive*   ___*negative*

Today, I honored my physical being by:

_____

_____

Today, I accomplished:

_____

_____

My choice to accomplish _____

supports the life I am trying to create by:

_____

_____

Today, I was most thankful for:

_____

_____

_____

_____

_____

_____

_____

_____

_____

_____

_____

_____

_____

_____

_____

Tomorrow, I intend to have a _____ *day, full*

of _____ *!*

Week5 | Day7 _____, 20_____

My mood this morning is: _____.

I slept: □ well   □ not well
             □ long enough   □ not long enough

My day is going to be: _____!

Evening Attitude Check: ___ *positive* ___*negative*

Today, I honored my physical being by:

_____

_____

Today, I accomplished:

_____

_____

My choice to accomplish _____

supports the life I am trying to create by:

_____

_____

Today, I was most thankful for:

_____

_____

_____

_____

_____

_____

_____

_____

_____

_____

_____

_____

_____

_____

Tomorrow, I intend to have a _____ **day, full**
of _____ **!**

Weekly Reflection #5

Each week you've been writing about the thing/moment you're most excited about in the week to come. How has this affected your outlook on the week? How do you think it affects your real-time gratitude in the actual moment you've been waiting for? Do you find yourself with more appreciation for the smaller things in life? Don't forget, you can and should be grateful for the unexpected! If you wish for something to have/happen in that week, write about your gratitude in advance!

_____

_____

_____

_____

_____

_____

_____

_____

_____

_____

_____

GRATITUDE IS WINE FOR THE SOUL. GO ON, GET DRUNK.

-RUMI

Week

6

_____ to _____

This week I am most excited about:

_____

_____

_____

_____

This week I plan to Thank Myself by:

_____

_____

_____

_____

Week6 | Day1 _____, 20_____

My mood this morning is: _____.

I slept: □ well   □ not well
             □ long enough   □ not long enough

My day is going to be: _____!

Evening Attitude Check: ___ *positive*   ___*negative*

Today, I honored my physical being by:

_____

_____

Today, I accomplished:

_____

_____

My choice to accomplish _____
supports the life I am trying to create by:

_____

_____

Today, I was most thankful for:

_____

_____

_____

_____

_____

_____

_____

_____

_____

_____

_____

_____

_____

_____

_____

Tomorrow, I intend to have a _____ *day, full of* _____ *!*

Week6 | Day2 _____, 20_____

My mood this morning is: _____.

I slept: □ well   □ not well
            □ long enough   □ not long enough

My day is going to be: _____!

Evening Attitude Check: ___ *positive* ___*negative*

Today, I honored my physical being by:

_____

_____

Today, I accomplished:

_____

_____

My choice to accomplish _____

supports the life I am trying to create by:

_____

_____

Today, I was most thankful for:

_____

_____

_____

_____

_____

_____

_____

_____

_____

_____

_____

_____

_____

_____

_____

Tomorrow, I intend to have a _____**day, full**

of_____**!**

Week6 | Day3 _____, 20_____

My mood this morning is: _____.

I slept: □ well   □ not well
             □ long enough   □ not long enough

My day is going to be: _____!

Evening Attitude Check: ___ *positive*   ___*negative*

Today, I honored my physical being by:

_____

_____

Today, I accomplished:

_____

_____

My choice to accomplish _____

supports the life I am trying to create by:

_____

_____

Today, I was most thankful for:

_____

_____

_____

_____

_____

_____

_____

_____

_____

_____

_____

_____

Tomorrow, I intend to have a _____ **day, full**
of _____ **!**

Week6 | Day4 _____, 20_____

My mood this morning is: _____.

I slept: □ well □ not well
          □ long enough □ not long enough

My day is going to be: _____!

Evening Attitude Check: ___ *positive* ___*negative*

Today, I honored my physical being by:

_____

_____

Today, I accomplished:

_____

_____

My choice to accomplish _____

supports the life I am trying to create by:

_____

_____

Today, I was most thankful for:

_____

_____

_____

_____

_____

_____

_____

_____

_____

_____

_____

_____

_____

Tomorrow, I intend to have a _____*day, full*

of _____*!*

Week6 | Day5 _____, 20_____

My mood this morning is: _____.

I slept: □ well   □ not well
          □ long enough   □ not long enough

My day is going to be: _____!

Evening Attitude Check: ___ *positive*   ___*negative*

Today, I honored my physical being by:

_____

_____

Today, I accomplished:

_____

_____

My choice to accomplish _____

supports the life I am trying to create by:

_____

_____

Today, I was most thankful for:

_____

_____

_____

_____

_____

_____

_____

_____

_____

_____

_____

_____

_____

_____

Tomorrow, I intend to have a _____ **day, full of** _____ **!**

Week6 | Day6   _____ , 20_____

My mood this morning is: _____ .

I slept: □ well   □ not well
                  □ long enough   □ not long enough

My day is going to be: _____ !

Evening Attitude Check: ___ *positive*   ___*negative*

Today, I honored my physical being by:

_____

_____

Today, I accomplished:

_____

_____

My choice to accomplish _____

supports the life I am trying to create by:

_____

_____

Today, I was most thankful for:

_____

_____

_____

_____

_____

_____

_____

_____

_____

_____

_____

_____

_____

_____

_____

Tomorrow, I intend to have a _____ **day, full**
of _____ **!**

Week6 | Day7 _____, 20_____

My mood this morning is: _____.

I slept: □ well   □ not well
             □ long enough   □ not long enough

My day is going to be: _____!

Evening Attitude Check: ___ *positive*   ___*negative*

Today, I honored my physical being by:

_____

_____

Today, I accomplished:

_____

_____

My choice to accomplish _____

supports the life I am trying to create by:

_____

_____

Today, I was most thankful for:

_____

_____

_____

_____

_____

_____

_____

_____

_____

_____

_____

_____

_____

_____

Tomorrow, I intend to have a _____ *day, full of* _____ *!*

Weekly Reflection #6

Part of self-determination is getting intentional about how we choose to fill our time. We all have the same 24 hours – does the way you currently spend your time help to create the life you desire? For six weeks now, you've notated awareness of your physical and mental energy. How do you feel this has affected your actions? Do you find yourself thinking about or creating new goals? Do you notice whether you engage more in short-term or long-term thinking when visualizing your ideals?

_____

_____

_____

_____

_____

_____

_____

_____

_____

_____

GRATITUDE DRIVES HAPPINESS
HAPPINESS BOOSTS PRODUCTIVITY
PRODUCTIVITY REVEALS MASTERY
AND MASTERY INSPIRES THE WORLD.

-ROBIN S. SHARMA

Week

7

_____ to _____

This week I am most excited about:

_____

_____

_____

_____

This week I plan to Thank Myself by:

_____

_____

_____

_____

Week7 | Day1   _____, 20_____

My mood this morning is: _____.

I slept: □ well   □ not well
                □ long enough   □ not long enough

My day is going to be: _____!

Evening Attitude Check: ___ *positive*   ___*negative*

Today, I honored my physical being by:

_____

_____

Today, I accomplished:

_____

_____

My choice to accomplish _____

supports the life I am trying to create by:

_____

_____

Today, I was most thankful for:

_____

_____

_____

_____

_____

_____

_____

_____

_____

_____

_____

_____

_____

_____

Tomorrow, I intend to have a _____ **day, full**
of _____ **!**

Week7 | Day2 _____, 20_____

My mood this morning is: _____.

I slept: □ well   □ not well
                  □ long enough   □ not long enough

My day is going to be: _____!

Evening Attitude Check: ___ *positive*   ___*negative*

Today, I honored my physical being by:

_____

_____

Today, I accomplished:

_____

_____

My choice to accomplish _____

supports the life I am trying to create by:

_____

_____

Today, I was most thankful for:

_____

_____

_____

_____

_____

_____

_____

_____

_____

_____

_____

_____

_____

_____

Tomorrow, I intend to have a _____**day, full**

of _____**!**

Week7 | Day3 _____, 20_____

My mood this morning is: _____.

I slept: □ well   □ not well
             □ long enough   □ not long enough

My day is going to be: _____!

Evening Attitude Check: ___ *positive*   ___*negative*

Today, I honored my physical being by:

_____

_____

Today, I accomplished:

_____

_____

My choice to accomplish _____

supports the life I am trying to create by:

_____

_____

Today, I was most thankful for:

_____

_____

_____

_____

_____

_____

_____

_____

_____

_____

_____

_____

_____

_____

_____

Tomorrow, I intend to have a _____ *day, full*
of _____ *!*

Week7 | Day4 _____, 20_____

My mood this morning is: _____.

I slept: □ well   □ not well
             □ long enough   □ not long enough

My day is going to be: _____!

Evening Attitude Check: ___ *positive*   ___*negative*

Today, I honored my physical being by:

_____

_____

Today, I accomplished:

_____

_____

My choice to accomplish _____

supports the life I am trying to create by:

_____

_____

Today, I was most thankful for:

_____

_____

_____

_____

_____

_____

_____

_____

_____

_____

_____

_____

_____

_____

Tomorrow, I intend to have a _____ **day, full**
of _____ **!**

Week7 | Day5 _____, 20_____

My mood this morning is: _____.

I slept: □ well   □ not well
               □ long enough   □ not long enough

My day is going to be: _____!

Evening Attitude Check: ___ *positive*   ___*negative*

Today, I honored my physical being by:

_____

_____

Today, I accomplished:

_____

_____

My choice to accomplish _____

supports the life I am trying to create by:

_____

_____

Today, I was most thankful for:

_____

_____

_____

_____

_____

_____

_____

_____

_____

_____

_____

_____

_____

_____

Tomorrow, I intend to have a _____ *day, full of* _____ *!*

Week7 | Day6 _____, 20_____

My mood this morning is: _____.

I slept: □ well □ not well
          □ long enough □ not long enough

My day is going to be: _____!

Evening Attitude Check: ___ positive ___negative

Today, I honored my physical being by:

_____

_____

Today, I accomplished:

_____

_____

My choice to accomplish _____

supports the life I am trying to create by:

_____

_____

Today, I was most thankful for:

_____

_____

_____

_____

_____

_____

_____

_____

_____

_____

_____

_____

_____

Tomorrow, I intend to have a _____ **day, full**
of _____ **!**

Week7 | Day7 _____, 20_____

My mood this morning is: _____.

I slept: □ well   □ not well
                      □ long enough   □ not long enough

My day is going to be: _____!

Evening Attitude Check: ___ *positive*   ___*negative*

Today, I honored my physical being by:

_____

_____

Today, I accomplished:

_____

_____

My choice to accomplish _____

supports the life I am trying to create by:

_____

_____

Today, I was most thankful for:

_____

_____

_____

_____

_____

_____

_____

_____

_____

_____

_____

_____

_____

_____

Tomorrow, I intend to have a _____ **day, full**
of _____ **!**

Weekly Reflection #7

Now that you're more than half-way through, compare your ease of recalling "thankfuls" to that of your first few weeks. Are you challenged to think of three? Do you ever use anything from your reserves list? Do you use all the writing space? (If you need extra, continue on in your NOTES in the back) You may have started out being thankful for family, friends, and good weather. As you move on, try to tune-in to some less obvious moments. Remember things that made you smile big. Recall things you'd normally take for granted that served you well. Notice when someone is especially kind. The more you write about and recall each of your items, the more impactful that memory is on your general perspective.

_____

_____

_____

_____

_____

_____

_____

_____

_____

AS WE EXPRESS OUR GRATITUDE,
WE MUST NEVER FORGET, THAT THE HIGHEST APPRECIATION IS NOT TO
UTTER THE WORDS, BUT TO LIVE BY THEM.

-JOHN F. KENNEDY

Week

8

_____ to _____

This week I am most excited about:

_____

_____

_____

_____

This week I plan to Thank Myself by:

_____

_____

_____

_____

Week8 | Day1 _____, 20_____

My mood this morning is: _____.

I slept: □ well   □ not well
             □ long enough   □ not long enough

My day is going to be: _____!

Evening Attitude Check: ___ *positive* ___*negative*

Today, I honored my physical being by:

_____

_____

Today, I accomplished:

_____

_____

My choice to accomplish _____

supports the life I am trying to create by:

_____

_____

Today, I was most thankful for:

_____

_____

_____

_____

_____

_____

_____

_____

_____

_____

_____

_____

_____

_____

Tomorrow, I intend to have a _____*day, full of* _____ *!*

Week8 | Day2 _____, 20_____

My mood this morning is: _____.

I slept: □ well   □ not well
                  □ long enough   □ not long enough

My day is going to be: _____!

Evening Attitude Check: ___ *positive* ___*negative*

Today, I honored my physical being by:

_____

_____

Today, I accomplished:

_____

_____

My choice to accomplish _____

supports the life I am trying to create by:

_____

_____

Today, I was most thankful for:

_____

_____

_____

_____

_____

_____

_____

_____

_____

_____

_____

_____

_____

_____

_____

Tomorrow, I intend to have a _____ **day, full**
of _____ **!**

Week8 | Day3 _____, 20_____

My mood this morning is: _____.

I slept: □ well   □ not well
                 □ long enough   □ not long enough

My day is going to be: _____!

Evening Attitude Check: ___ *positive*   ___*negative*

Today, I honored my physical being by:

_____

_____

Today, I accomplished:

_____

_____

My choice to accomplish _____

supports the life I am trying to create by:

_____

_____

Today, I was most thankful for:

_____

_____

_____

_____

_____

_____

_____

_____

_____

_____

_____

_____

_____

Tomorrow, I intend to have a _____**day, full**
of _____**!**

Week8 | Day4 _____, 20_____

My mood this morning is: _____.

I slept: □ well   □ not well

                □ long enough   □ not long enough

My day is going to be: _____!

Evening Attitude Check: ___ *positive* ___*negative*

Today, I honored my physical being by:

_____

_____

Today, I accomplished:

_____

_____

My choice to accomplish _____

supports the life I am trying to create by:

_____

_____

Today, I was most thankful for:

_____

_____

_____

_____

_____

_____

_____

_____

_____

_____

_____

_____

_____

_____

Tomorrow, I intend to have a _____ *day, full of* _____ *!*

Week8 | Day5 _____, 20_____

My mood this morning is: _____.

I slept: □ well   □ not well
          □ long enough   □ not long enough

My day is going to be: _____!

Evening Attitude Check: ___ *positive*   ___*negative*

Today, I honored my physical being by:

_____

_____

Today, I accomplished:

_____

_____

My choice to accomplish _____

supports the life I am trying to create by:

_____

_____

Today, I was most thankful for:

_____

_____

_____

_____

_____

_____

_____

_____

_____

_____

_____

_____

_____

_____

Tomorrow, I intend to have a _____ *day, full*
of _____ *!*

Week8 | Day6 _____, 20_____

My mood this morning is: _____.

I slept: □ well   □ not well
             □ long enough   □ not long enough

My day is going to be: _____!

Evening Attitude Check: ___ *positive*   ___*negative*

Today, I honored my physical being by:

_____

_____

Today, I accomplished:

_____

_____

My choice to accomplish _____

supports the life I am trying to create by:

_____

_____

Today, I was most thankful for:

_____

_____

_____

_____

_____

_____

_____

_____

_____

_____

_____

_____

_____

_____

_____

Tomorrow, I intend to have a _____ **day, full**

of _____ **!**

Week8 | Day7   _____, 20_____

My mood this morning is: _____.

I slept: □ well   □ not well
                □ long enough   □ not long enough

My day is going to be: _____!

Evening Attitude Check: ___ *positive*   ___*negative*

Today, I honored my physical being by:

_____

_____

Today, I accomplished:

_____

_____

My choice to accomplish _____

supports the life I am trying to create by:

_____

_____

Today, I was most thankful for:

_____

_____

_____

_____

_____

_____

_____

_____

_____

_____

_____

_____

_____

_____

Tomorrow, I intend to have a _____ *day, full of* _____ *!*

Weekly Reflection #8

Life gets busy. Sometimes we're tired. Sometimes you have a
no-good-crummy day and it's all you can do to order dinner.
These are the times we need Gratitude Triggers. A Gratitude
Trigger is anything you can look at or "stumble upon" that
gives you an instant smile and immediate hope. Gratitude has
the ability to interrupt and correct negative thought patterns, so
it is important to build triggers into your life - in your playlist,
on your desk at work, in your gym bag - anywhere that has a
continual and significant presence in your days. What item(s)
can you use as your gratitude triggers and how will you build
them into your days? (if you need ideas, see the Gratitude
Triggers section in the back!)

_____

_____

_____

_____

_____

_____

_____

_____

_____

WHEN YOU PRACTICE GRATEFULNESS,
THERE IS A SENSE OF RESPECT TOWARD OTHERS.

-DALAI LAMA

Week

9

_____ to _____

This week I am most excited about:

_____

_____

_____

_____

This week I plan to Thank Myself by:

_____

_____

_____

_____

Week9 | Day1 _____, 20_____

My mood this morning is: _____.

I slept: □ well   □ not well
          □ long enough   □ not long enough

My day is going to be: _____!

Evening Attitude Check: ___ *positive*   ___*negative*

Today, I honored my physical being by:

_____

_____

Today, I accomplished:

_____

_____

My choice to accomplish _____
supports the life I am trying to create by:

_____

_____

Today, I was most thankful for:

_____

_____

_____

_____

_____

_____

_____

_____

_____

_____

_____

_____

_____

_____

_____

Tomorrow, I intend to have a _____ *day, full of* _____ *!*

Week9 | Day2   _____, 20_____

My mood this morning is: _____.

I slept: □ well   □ not well
                 □ long enough   □ not long enough

My day is going to be: _____!

Evening Attitude Check: ___ *positive*   ___*negative*

Today, I honored my physical being by:

_____

_____

Today, I accomplished:

_____

_____

My choice to accomplish _____

supports the life I am trying to create by:

_____

_____

Today, I was most thankful for:

_____

_____

_____

_____

_____

_____

_____

_____

_____

_____

_____

_____

_____

_____

_____

Tomorrow, I intend to have a _____ *day, full of* _____ *!*

Week9 | Day3   _____, 20_____

My mood this morning is: _____.

I slept: □ well   □ not well
                □ long enough   □ not long enough

My day is going to be: _____!

Evening Attitude Check: ___ *positive*   ___*negative*

Today, I honored my physical being by:

_____

_____

Today, I accomplished:

_____

_____

My choice to accomplish _____

supports the life I am trying to create by:

_____

_____

Today, I was most thankful for:

_____

_____

_____

_____

_____

_____

_____

_____

_____

_____

_____

_____

_____

_____

Tomorrow, I intend to have a _____ **day, full of** _____ **!**

Week9 | Day4 _____, 20_____

My mood this morning is: _____.

I slept: □ well   □ not well
      □ long enough □ not long enough

My day is going to be: _____!

Evening Attitude Check: ___ *positive* ___*negative*

Today, I honored my physical being by:

_____

_____

Today, I accomplished:

_____

_____

My choice to accomplish _____

supports the life I am trying to create by:

_____

_____

Today, I was most thankful for:

_____

_____

_____

_____

_____

_____

_____

_____

_____

_____

_____

_____

_____

_____

Tomorrow, I intend to have a _____ *day, full of* _____ *!*

Week9 | Day5 _____, 20_____

My mood this morning is: _____.

I slept: □ well   □ not well
          □ long enough   □ not long enough

My day is going to be: _____!

Evening Attitude Check: ___ *positive*   ___*negative*

Today, I honored my physical being by:

_____

_____

Today, I accomplished:

_____

_____

My choice to accomplish _____

supports the life I am trying to create by:

_____

_____

Today, I was most thankful for:

_____

_____

_____

_____

_____

_____

_____

_____

_____

_____

_____

_____

_____

_____

Tomorrow, I intend to have a _____ **day, full**

of _____**!**

Week9 | Day6 _____, 20_____

My mood this morning is: _____.

I slept: □ well   □ not well
             □ long enough   □ not long enough

My day is going to be: _____!

Evening Attitude Check: ___ *positive*   ___*negative*

Today, I honored my physical being by:

_____

_____

Today, I accomplished:

_____

_____

My choice to accomplish _____
supports the life I am trying to create by:

_____

_____

Today, I was most thankful for:

_____

_____

_____

_____

_____

_____

_____

_____

_____

_____

_____

_____

_____

_____

Tomorrow, I intend to have a _____ day, full of _____!

Week9 | Day7   _____, 20_____

My mood this morning is: _____.

I slept: □ well   □ not well
                 □ long enough   □ not long enough

My day is going to be: _____!

Evening Attitude Check: ___ *positive*   ___*negative*

Today, I honored my physical being by:

_____

_____

Today, I accomplished:

_____

_____

My choice to accomplish _____

supports the life I am trying to create by:

_____

_____

Today, I was most thankful for:

_____

_____

_____

_____

_____

_____

_____

_____

_____

_____

_____

_____

_____

_____

Tomorrow, I intend to have a _____ *day, full*
of _____ *!*

Weekly Reflection #9

Gratitude is *Love in Action.* Love in Action spreads Joy!

Over the past nine weeks, do you notice yourself being more aware of how you outwardly express your gratitude? In what ways have you turned your gratitude into action? How do you plan to integrate some actions into your daily life going forward? (If you need some ideas, see the "Gratitude in Action" section in the back!)

_____

_____

_____

_____

_____

_____

_____

_____

_____

_____

THE WAY TO MOVE OUT OF JUDGEMENT IS TO MOVE INTO GRATITUDE.

-NEALE DONALD WALSCH

Week

10

_____ to _____

This week I am most excited about:

_____

_____

_____

_____

This week I plan to Thank Myself by:

_____

_____

_____

_____

Week10 | Day1   _____, 20_____

My mood this morning is: _____.

I slept: □ well   □ not well
                □ long enough   □ not long enough

My day is going to be: _____!

Evening Attitude Check: ___ *positive*   ___*negative*

Today, I honored my physical being by:

_____

_____

Today, I accomplished:

_____

_____

My choice to accomplish _____

supports the life I am trying to create by:

_____

_____

Today, I was most thankful for:

_____

_____

_____

_____

_____

_____

_____

_____

_____

_____

_____

_____

_____

_____

Tomorrow, I intend to have a _____ *day, full*
of _____ *!*

Week10 | Day2 _____, 20_____

My mood this morning is: _____.

I slept: □ well   □ not well
                    □ long enough   □ not long enough

My day is going to be: _____!

Evening Attitude Check: ___ *positive* ___ *negative*

Today, I honored my physical being by:

_____

_____

Today, I accomplished:

_____

_____

My choice to accomplish _____

supports the life I am trying to create by:

_____

_____

Today, I was most thankful for:

_____

_____
_____
_____
_____

_____
_____
_____
_____
_____

_____
_____
_____
_____
_____

Tomorrow, I intend to have a _____ *day, full*
of _____ *!*

Week10 | Day3 _____, 20_____

My mood this morning is: _____.

I slept: □ well   □ not well
             □ long enough   □ not long enough

My day is going to be: _____!

Evening Attitude Check: ___ *positive*   ___*negative*

Today, I honored my physical being by:

_____

_____

Today, I accomplished:

_____

_____

My choice to accomplish _____

supports the life I am trying to create by:

_____

_____

Today, I was most thankful for:

_____

_____

_____

_____

_____

_____

_____

_____

_____

_____

_____

_____

_____

Tomorrow, I intend to have a _____**day, full**
of_____**!**

Week10 | Day4 _____, 20_____

My mood this morning is: _____.

I slept: □ well □ not well
□ long enough □ not long enough

My day is going to be: _____!

Evening Attitude Check: ___ *positive* ___*negative*

Today, I honored my physical being by:

_____

_____

Today, I accomplished:

_____

_____

My choice to accomplish _____

supports the life I am trying to create by:

_____

_____

Today, I was most thankful for:

_____

_____

_____

_____

_____

_____

_____

_____

_____

_____

_____

_____

_____

_____

Tomorrow, I intend to have a _____*day, full*
of _____*!*

Week10 | Day5 _____, 20_____

My mood this morning is: _____.

I slept: □ well   □ not well
          □ long enough   □ not long enough

My day is going to be: _____!

Evening Attitude Check: ___ *positive*   ___*negative*

Today, I honored my physical being by:

_____

_____

Today, I accomplished:

_____

_____

My choice to accomplish _____

supports the life I am trying to create by:

_____

_____

Today, I was most thankful for:

_____

_____

_____

_____

_____

_____

_____

_____

_____

_____

_____

_____

_____

_____

Tomorrow, I intend to have a _____ **day, full of** _____ **!**

Week10 | Day6 _____, 20_____

My mood this morning is: _____.

I slept: □ well   □ not well
                      □ long enough   □ not long enough

My day is going to be: _____!

Evening Attitude Check: ___ *positive*   ___*negative*

Today, I honored my physical being by:

_____

_____

Today, I accomplished:

_____

_____

My choice to accomplish _____

supports the life I am trying to create by:

_____

_____

Today, I was most thankful for:

_____

_____

_____

_____

_____

_____

_____

_____

_____

_____

_____

_____

_____

_____

Tomorrow, I intend to have a _____**day, full**
of _____**!**

Week10 | Day7 _____, 20_____

My mood this morning is: _____.

I slept: □ well   □ not well
                 □ long enough   □ not long enough

My day is going to be: _____!

Evening Attitude Check: ___ positive   ___negative

Today, I honored my physical being by:

_____

_____

Today, I accomplished:

_____

_____

My choice to accomplish _____

supports the life I am trying to create by:

_____

_____

Today, I was most thankful for:

_____

_____

_____

_____

_____

_____

_____

_____

_____

_____

_____

_____

_____

_____

Tomorrow, I intend to have a _____ *day, full of* _____ *!*

The Gratitude Mirror

At any given time, there may be at least one major component that you're not happy with. You like your job, but your boss treats you unfairly. Your home is not fancy and could use some repairs. You haven't had a date night in ages, because *Life*. Whatever it is, you can usually turn it around.

> *Laundry means your home is full.* Maybe you had the money to buy those clothes, and maybe you have a washing machine.
>
> *Dishes mean your loved ones have eaten.* Maybe you had the money to buy that food, and maybe you have a dishwasher.
>
> *An awful boss means you have a job.* You have the opportunity to earn a paycheck while you are looking for other employment.
>
> *That fight with your sibling?* You have at least one person in this world who cares enough to argue with you.

Think of something that is either upsetting to you now or has bothered you recently. Write about the issue/person/situation here:

_____

_____

_____

_____

_____

_____

NOW, use your Gratitude Mirror to reflect all the good in the situation, and write about it here:

_____

_____

_____

_____

_____

_____

_____

_____

_____

_____

_____

_____

_____

_____

_____

_____

GIVE THANKS
FOR EACH NEW MORNING WITH ITS LIGHT
FOR REST AND SHELTER OF THE NIGHT
FOR HEALTH AND FOOD; FOR LOVE AND FRIENDS
FOR EVERYTHING THY GOODNESS SENDS.
-RALPH WALDO EMERSON

Week

11

_____ to _____

This week I am most excited about:

_____

_____

_____

_____

This week I plan to Thank Myself by:

_____

_____

_____

_____

Week11 | Day1 _____, 20_____

My mood this morning is: _____.

I slept: □ well   □ not well
          □ long enough   □ not long enough

My day is going to be: _____!

Evening Attitude Check: ___ *positive*   ___*negative*

Today, I honored my physical being by:

_____

_____

Today, I accomplished:

_____

_____

My choice to accomplish _____
supports the life I am trying to create by:

_____

_____

Today, I was most thankful for:

_____

_____

_____

_____

_____

_____

_____

_____

_____

_____

_____

_____

_____

_____

Tomorrow, I intend to have a _____ *day, full*
of _____ *!*

Week11 | Day2   _____, 20_____

My mood this morning is: _____.

I slept: □ well   □ not well
                □ long enough   □ not long enough

My day is going to be: _____!

Evening Attitude Check: ___ *positive*   ___*negative*

Today, I honored my physical being by:

_____

_____

Today, I accomplished:

_____

_____

My choice to accomplish _____

supports the life I am trying to create by:

_____

_____

Today, I was most thankful for:

_____

_____

_____

_____

_____

_____

_____

_____

_____

_____

_____

_____

_____

_____

Tomorrow, I intend to have a _____ *day, full*
of _____ *!*

Week11 | Day3 _____, 20_____

My mood this morning is: _____.

I slept: □ well   □ not well
             □ long enough   □ not long enough

My day is going to be: _____!

Evening Attitude Check: ___ *positive*   ___*negative*

Today, I honored my physical being by:

_____

_____

Today, I accomplished:

_____

_____

My choice to accomplish _____

supports the life I am trying to create by:

_____

_____

Today, I was most thankful for:

_____

_____

_____

_____

_____

_____

_____

_____

_____

_____

_____

_____

_____

Tomorrow, I intend to have a _____ *day, full of* _____*!*

Week11 | Day4 _____, 20_____

My mood this morning is: _____.

I slept: □ well   □ not well
              □ long enough   □ not long enough

My day is going to be: _____!

Evening Attitude Check: ___ *positive*   ___*negative*

Today, I honored my physical being by:

_____

_____

Today, I accomplished:

_____

_____

My choice to accomplish _____

supports the life I am trying to create by:

_____

_____

Today, I was most thankful for:

_____

_____

_____

_____

_____

_____

_____

_____

_____

_____

_____

_____

_____

_____

_____

Tomorrow, I intend to have a _____ *day, full*
of _____ *!*

Week11 | Day5 _____, 20_____

My mood this morning is: _____.

I slept: □ well   □ not well
                □ long enough   □ not long enough

My day is going to be: _____!

Evening Attitude Check: ___ *positive*   ___*negative*

Today, I honored my physical being by:

_____

_____

Today, I accomplished:

_____

_____

My choice to accomplish _____

supports the life I am trying to create by:

_____

_____

Today, I was most thankful for:

_____

_____

_____

_____

_____

_____

_____

_____

_____

_____

_____

_____

_____

_____

Tomorrow, I intend to have a _____ *day, full*
of _____ *!*

Week11 | Day6 _____, 20_____

My mood this morning is: _____.

I slept: □ well   □ not well
             □ long enough   □ not long enough

My day is going to be: _____!

Evening Attitude Check: ___ *positive*   ___*negative*

Today, I honored my physical being by:

_____

_____

Today, I accomplished:

_____

_____

My choice to accomplish _____

supports the life I am trying to create by:

_____

_____

Today, I was most thankful for:

_____
_____
_____
_____
_____

_____
_____
_____
_____
_____

_____
_____
_____
_____
_____

Tomorrow, I intend to have a _____ *day, full*
of _____*!*

Week11 | Day7 _____, 20_____

My mood this morning is: _____.

I slept: □ well   □ not well
                    □ long enough   □ not long enough

My day is going to be: _____!

Evening Attitude Check: ___ *positive* ___*negative*

Today, I honored my physical being by:

_____

_____

Today, I accomplished:

_____

_____

My choice to accomplish _____

supports the life I am trying to create by:

_____

_____

Today, I was most thankful for:

_____

_____

_____

_____

_____

_____

_____

_____

_____

_____

_____

_____

_____

Tomorrow, I intend to have a _____**day, full**

of _____**!**

Weekly Reflection #11

Energy is contagious. You may notice that you don't want to be around a person who is constantly complaining. The same logic applies to a grateful spirit – positive energy will begin to radiate effortlessly. It is almost impossible to feel anger in the same moment you're feeling gratitude. Gratitude sparks positive vibes, and positive vibes build positive people! How do you feel your journey has affected the people you choose to be around? How do you feel your journey has affected the people who choose YOU? Take a minute to reflect on the company you keep, and how you are spreading your goodness.

_____

_____

_____

_____

_____

_____

_____

_____

_____

_____

_____

GRATITUDE IS A CURRENCY WE CAN MINT FOR OURSELVES
AND SPEND WITHOUT FEAR OF BANKRUPTCY.

-FRED DE WITT VAN AMBURGH

Week

12

_____ to _____

This week I am most excited about:

_____

_____

_____

_____

This week I plan to Thank Myself by:

_____

_____

_____

_____

Week12 | Day1 _____, 20_____

My mood this morning is: _____.

I slept: □ well   □ not well
                       □ long enough   □ not long enough

My day is going to be: _____!

Evening Attitude Check: ___ *positive*   ___*negative*

Today, I honored my physical being by:

_____

_____

Today, I accomplished:

_____

_____

My choice to accomplish _____

supports the life I am trying to create by:

_____

_____

Today, I was most thankful for:

_____

_____

_____

_____

_____

_____

_____

_____

_____

_____

_____

_____

_____

_____

_____

Tomorrow, I intend to have a _____ *day, full*
of _____ *!*

Week12 | Day2 _____, 20_____

My mood this morning is: _____.

I slept: □ well   □ not well
          □ long enough   □ not long enough

My day is going to be: _____!

Evening Attitude Check: ___ *positive*   ___*negative*

Today, I honored my physical being by:

_____

_____

Today, I accomplished:

_____

_____

My choice to accomplish _____

supports the life I am trying to create by:

_____

_____

Today, I was most thankful for:

_____

_____

_____

_____

_____

_____

_____

_____

_____

_____

_____

_____

_____

_____

Tomorrow, I intend to have a _____**day, full**
of _____**!**

Week12 | Day3 _____, 20_____

My mood this morning is: _____.

I slept: □ well   □ not well
                   □ long enough   □ not long enough

My day is going to be: _____!

Evening Attitude Check: ___ *positive* ___*negative*

Today, I honored my physical being by:

_____

_____

Today, I accomplished:

_____

_____

My choice to accomplish _____

supports the life I am trying to create by:

_____

_____

Today, I was most thankful for:

_____

_____

_____

_____

_____

_____

_____

_____

_____

_____

_____

_____

_____

Tomorrow, I intend to have a _____**day, full**
of _____**!**

Week12 | Day4   _____, 20_____

My mood this morning is: _____.

I slept: □ well   □ not well
                □ long enough   □ not long enough

My day is going to be: _____!

Evening Attitude Check: ___ *positive*   ___*negative*

Today, I honored my physical being by:

_____

_____

Today, I accomplished:

_____

_____

My choice to accomplish _____

supports the life I am trying to create by:

_____

_____

Today, I was most thankful for:

_____

_____

_____

_____

_____

_____

_____

_____

_____

_____

_____

_____

_____

_____

Tomorrow, I intend to have a _____ *day, full*
of _____ *!*

Week12 | Day5 _____, 20_____

My mood this morning is: _____.

I slept: □ well □ not well
          □ long enough □ not long enough

My day is going to be: _____!

Evening Attitude Check: ___ *positive* ___*negative*

Today, I honored my physical being by:

_____

_____

Today, I accomplished:

_____

_____

My choice to accomplish _____

supports the life I am trying to create by:

_____

_____

Today, I was most thankful for:

_____

_____

_____

_____

_____

_____

_____

_____

_____

_____

_____

_____

_____

_____

_____

Tomorrow, I intend to have a _____ ***day, full***
of _____ ***!***

Week12 | Day6 _____, 20_____

My mood this morning is: _____.

I slept: □ well   □ not well
          □ long enough   □ not long enough

My day is going to be: _____!

Evening Attitude Check: ___ *positive*   ___ *negative*

Today, I honored my physical being by:

_____

_____

Today, I accomplished:

_____

_____

My choice to accomplish _____

supports the life I am trying to create by:

_____

_____

Today, I was most thankful for:

_____

_____

_____

_____

_____

_____

_____

_____

_____

_____

_____

_____

_____

_____

_____

Tomorrow, I intend to have a _____ day, full of _____ !

Week12 | Day7   _____, 20_____

My mood this morning is: _____.

I slept: □ well   □ not well
                □ long enough   □ not long enough

My day is going to be: _____!

Evening Attitude Check: ___ *positive*   ___*negative*

Today, I honored my physical being by:

_____

_____

Today, I accomplished:

_____

_____

My choice to accomplish _____

supports the life I am trying to create by:

_____

_____

Today, I was most thankful for:

_____

_____

_____

_____

_____

_____

_____

_____

_____

_____

_____

_____

_____

_____

Tomorrow, I intend to have a _____*day, full*
of _____*!*

Weekly Reflection #12

Think about your hopes when beginning this journey. Were there particulars you wanted to change? Did you have ideas about how this would make you feel? Did you have pre-determined thoughts about how long you would last, or if you would continue the practice once the journal was complete? How often do you find yourself in a place of gratitude? Have you had the opportunity and success with using gratitude to divert your feelings during a difficult situation? List some ways this practice has affected the way you live your life:

_____

_____

_____

_____

_____

_____

_____

_____

_____

_____

THERE IS NO JOY WITHOUT GRATITUDE.

-BRENE BROWN

Week

13

_____ to _____

This week I am most excited about:

_____

_____

_____

_____

This week I plan to Thank Myself by:

_____

_____

_____

_____

Week13 | Day1 _____, 20_____

My mood this morning is: _____.

I slept: □ well   □ not well
            □ long enough   □ not long enough

My day is going to be: _____!

Evening Attitude Check: ___ *positive* ___*negative*

Today, I honored my physical being by:

_____

_____

Today, I accomplished:

_____

_____

My choice to accomplish _____

supports the life I am trying to create by:

_____

_____

Today, I was most thankful for:

_____

_____

_____

_____

_____

_____

_____

_____

_____

_____

_____

_____

_____

_____

Tomorrow, I intend to have a _____**day, full**

of _____**!**

Week13 | Day2 _____, 20_____

My mood this morning is: _____.

I slept: □ well   □ not well
             □ long enough   □ not long enough

My day is going to be: _____!

Evening Attitude Check: ___ *positive* ___*negative*

Today, I honored my physical being by:

_____

_____

Today, I accomplished:

_____

_____

My choice to accomplish _____

supports the life I am trying to create by:

_____

_____

Today, I was most thankful for:

_____

_____

_____

_____

_____

_____

_____

_____

_____

_____

_____

_____

_____

_____

Tomorrow, I intend to have a _____ *day, full
of* _____ *!*

Week13 | Day3 _____, 20_____

My mood this morning is: _____.

I slept: □ well   □ not well
          □ long enough   □ not long enough

My day is going to be: _____!

Evening Attitude Check: ___ *positive*   ___*negative*

Today, I honored my physical being by:

_____

_____

Today, I accomplished:

_____

_____

My choice to accomplish _____

supports the life I am trying to create by:

_____

_____

Today, I was most thankful for:

_____

_____

_____

_____

_____

_____

_____

_____

_____

_____

_____

_____

_____

_____

Tomorrow, I intend to have a _____*day, full of* _____*!*

Week13 | Day4 _____, 20_____

My mood this morning is: _____.

I slept: □ well   □ not well
             □ long enough   □ not long enough

My day is going to be: _____!

Evening Attitude Check: ___ *positive*   ___*negative*

Today, I honored my physical being by:

_____

_____

Today, I accomplished:

_____

_____

My choice to accomplish _____

supports the life I am trying to create by:

_____

_____

Today, I was most thankful for:

_____

_____

_____

_____

_____

_____

_____

_____

_____

_____

_____

_____

_____

_____

Tomorrow, I intend to have a _____ **day, full**
of _____ **!**

Week13 | Day5 _____, 20_____

My mood this morning is: _____.

I slept: □ well   □ not well
             □ long enough   □ not long enough

My day is going to be: _____!

Evening Attitude Check: ___ *positive*   ___*negative*

Today, I honored my physical being by:

_____

_____

Today, I accomplished:

_____

_____

My choice to accomplish _____

supports the life I am trying to create by:

_____

_____

Today, I was most thankful for:

_____

_____

_____

_____

_____

_____

_____

_____

_____

_____

_____

_____

_____

_____

Tomorrow, I intend to have a _____ *day, full*

of _____ *!*

Week13 | Day6 _____, 20_____

My mood this morning is: _____.

I slept: □ well □ not well
□ long enough □ not long enough

My day is going to be: _____!

Evening Attitude Check: ___ *positive* ___*negative*

Today, I honored my physical being by:

_____

_____

Today, I accomplished:

_____

_____

My choice to accomplish _____

supports the life I am trying to create by:

_____

_____

Today, I was most thankful for:

_____

_____

_____

_____

_____

_____

_____

_____

_____

_____

_____

_____

_____

_____

_____

Tomorrow, I intend to have a _____ **day, full**

of _____ **!**

Week13 | Day7   _____, 20_____

My mood this morning is: _____.

I slept: □ well   □ not well
                 □ long enough   □ not long enough

My day is going to be: _____!

Evening Attitude Check: ___ *positive*   ___*negative*

Today, I honored my physical being by:

_____

_____

Today, I accomplished:

_____

_____

My choice to accomplish _____

supports the life I am trying to create by:

_____

_____

Today, I was most thankful for:

_____

_____

_____

_____

_____

_____

_____

_____

_____

_____

_____

_____

_____

_____

Tomorrow, I intend to have a _____**day, full**
of _____**!**

Letter to ME

Use your reflections from week 12 to write yourself a letter. First acknowledge where you came from (awareness is key!), recognize any and all positive changes you've made, and celebrate where you are today! Continued practice of any habit will create a lifestyle, and a lifestyle of gratitude can be life-changing!

_____

_____

_____

_____

_____

_____

_____

_____

_____

_____

_____

GRATITUDE TRIGGERS

Possibilities:

- Family Photos
- Vacation Keepsakes
- Favorite Quotes
- Children's Artwork
- Small trinkets that make you smile
- Inspirational Playlists
- Candles/Oils/etc to infuse your environment with your favorite scents
- Books & Poetry that inspire you
- A card or letter that someone sent you
- Nostalgic Memoires
- Thank-you sticky notes
- Use a dry-erase marker to write affirmations on windows or mirrors
- Self-curated screensavers
- Cozy throw blankets

GRATITUDE in ACTION!

Ideas for blessing others with your own gratitude:

- o   Send a card or handwritten note.
- o   "Pay it forward" in line.
- o   Bring someone coffee.
- o   Look a stranger in the eyes and smile.
- o   Ask someone about the best part of their day.
- o   Mow the neighbor's lawn.
- o   Take someone's children for a playdate.
- o   Give someone an extra-long hug.
- o   Deliver flowers just to brighten someone's day.
- o   Offer to return someone's shopping cart.
- o   Compliment 5 random people.
- o   Have dinner delivered to someone who's been busy (everyone likes pizza!)
- o   Bring tea, cough drops, magazines, etc. to someone who's feeling under the weather.
- o   Find one thing you can do to lighten someone's load today.

NOTES

NOTES

NOTES

NOTES

NOTES

NOTES

NOTES

NOTES

NOTES

NOTES

NOTES

NOTES

NOTES

NOTES

NOTES

NOTES

NOTES

NOTES

NOTES

NOTES

About the Author

Gina Low is a mom, wife, kid-sports cheerleader, and wine taster who swears that the *40s* are the best years of her life – because, *Gratitude*.

She blogs at *She's Overflowing* for all you fellow warriors who may have temporarily lost yourselves in the throes of spit up and goldfish. By the grace of GRATITUDE, she will help guide you through the years of cleats, cups (every cup but sippy cups anymore), and collective bargaining with teens; all while reminding you that <u>your oxygen mask must come first</u>.

You can also join Gina and other gratitude junkies on the Facebook page "She's Overflowing", and in its group designed specifically for you: #gratitudegains

Made in the USA
Monee, IL
11 December 2020